MW01614846

Ask a

Master

Volume 1

By Bill FitzPatrick

Although the American Success Institute has researched many sources to ensure the accuracy and completeness of the information contained in this book, the Institute cannot accept any responsibility for errors, inaccuracies, omissions, or any other inconsistency herein. Any slights against people or organizations are unintentional.

Ask a Master, Volume 1. Copyright © 2001 by the American Success Institute, Inc. All rights reserved. No part of this book may be reproduced or transmitted in any form or by any means, electronic or mechanical, including photocopying, recording, or by any information storage and retrieval system, without permission in writing from the American Success Institute, Inc.

ASK A MASTER, VOLUME 1™, THE MASTER'S MEDITATION MANTRAS, VOLUME 1™, 100 ACTION PRINCIPLES ™, MASTER SUCCESS ™, 100 ACTION PRINCIPLES OF THE SHAOLIN ™, POSITIVE MENTAL ATTITUDES ™, AFRICAN-AMERICANS ON SUCCESS ™, SPORTS LEGENDS ON SUCCESS ™, WINNING WITH SMALL BUSINESS ™, TENGA UNA ACTITUD MENTAL POSITIVA ™, WOMEN ON SUCCESS ™, SPORTS LEGENDS ON SUCCESS ™ and ATTITUDES MENTALES POSITIVES ™ are all trademarks of the American Success Institute, Inc.

Educational and motivational materials from the American Success Institute are available at special discounts for bulk purchases. For additional information, contact:

American Success Institute
5 North Main Street
Natick, MA 01760
www.dojo.com

Phone: 1-800-585-1300

e-mail: info@dojo.com

Illustrated by Sam Valentino. Cover, book design, typography, and electronic pagination by Painted Turtle Productions, Newton, MA.

Printed in the United States of America

ISBN 1-884864-17-1
Library of Congress Catalog Card Number: 2001 135171

Table of Contents

Introduction

You read the Action Principles and agree with the philosophy and you think, "OK, now what?" This is the reason for *Ask A Master*. Yes, in theory, you want to improve yourself. Yes, in theory, you want to help others. But, how do these theories translate to the challenges and opportunities presented by daily life? The questions and answers give you an opportunity to consider my advice as related to all of your major goal areas: spiritual, family, physical, career, cultural, community, social, intellectual, investment and your personal goals.

As with all the Shaolin Master materials presented on Dojo.com, the intent of the answers is not to command but rather to serve as a basis for you to consider your own opinions and choose your own best courses of action. Remember, Shaolin Masters are only teachers. You must research. You must think. You must act. You must learn. You must teach others.

On the "Be a Shaolin Master" posters one of the characteristics listed is to "Seek Simple Solutions." It is important to realize that by simple I am not implying that solutions be simplistic or even easy. Many simple answers will require both hard work and sacrifice. For example, if you want a comfortable retirement, save 10% of your income. If you want a comfortable early retirement, save 20% of your income. If you want to retire early and wealthy, buy six income properties. If you want to be popular, listen more, remember names and help others. If you want to be healthier, eat less and exercise more. These are simple solutions but not easy solutions. Many of the answers are simple, direct and action oriented but take a tough persistent person to implement. But, of course, you are that person. You are an Action Principles champion.

As with the Master's Meditation Mantras, these questions and answers, especially those presenting moral dilemmas, can be used by teachers, counselors and parents to encourage discussion. Students can be asked to agree or disagree with the answers and to express and defend their viewpoints.

I hope you enjoy this collection and our other offerings on Dojo.com. If you do, please tell others. Thank you.

Bill FitzPatrick
A Shaolin Master

5

1.
Looking for my soul mate

I am 37 years old and not having much success meeting my soul mate. I don't think that I'm a very interesting person. What would the Shaolin Master say?

Shaolin Master: Start by doing things you love and you may find someone to love. Talk about your interests and you'll be interesting. Do you love gardening? Join a garden club. Do you love to travel, hike, read? There are clubs and associations and groups where you can meet others with a common interest.

2.
Too much time online

My 15-year-old son spends all his time at home on the Internet. I know that he is neglecting his schoolwork. When I confront him, he gets abusive. How should I punish him?

Shaolin Master: You can punish a five-year-old. You have to reason with a fifteen-year-old. Is he willing to admit that the Internet is affecting his schoolwork? Is he willing to self-impose reasonable limits on himself so that the schoolwork gets done? Will he concede that poor grades will have a long-term negative impact on his own life? You want your son to admit that a problem exists and you want him to accept responsibility for solving the problem. If you can speak civilly to each other, you have a chance at a satisfactory resolution. If your son remains in denial and is abusive, your problems have escalated beyond the Internet situation and you may have to seek professional assistance. If his schoolwork is suffering, the school may be willing to suggest appropriate counseling.

3.
Hiring my brother-in-law

My wife's brother has a very poor work history and is broke and out of a job again. I own a small retail business and my wife wants me to hire him. He's not a bad guy and he is family. What should I do?

Shaolin Master: From your question, you already know what to do – don't hire him! You don't need his problems to become your problems. I'm sure you're busy and the last thing you want to do is to start baby-sitting this fellow who may start thinking that he is an entitled person being "family." Stay well clear of this one. Give him a copy of *The Action Principles,* tell him how much the book has helped you and suggest that he read the book and come back in a week and you will discuss with him how the APs might help him to find a better life. Chances are he'll run the other way. If he does come back with a positive attitude, help him find a job, but elsewhere. If your wife continues to feel sorry for him, even lending him a few bucks will be short money compared to hiring him and worrying about his performance every day.

4.
Shaolin Kempo versus Aikido

I am not a very aggressive type person and I want to study a martial art. A friend told me that Aikido would be better for me since it is a much gentler martial art than Shaolin Kempo. Is this correct?

Shaolin Master: If you are training by yourself, both styles are safe and relatively gentle. If you are working out in the dojo with a partner in a class, both styles are safe and relatively gentle. If you are in need of self-defense, both styles are effective. Yes, many times, Shaolin Kempo can look like street fighting to an outsider. Yes, many times, Aikido performed by experts can look like gentle tumbling to an outsider. However, if a skilled Aikido practitioner were to flip a mugger, that mugger would not know how to gently tumble and would land on his head. Which is gentler, to be flipped in Aikido or punched in Kempo? It is your attitude and self-discipline that makes you gentle or rough, not the style of martial art.

5.
Not enough hours

I work sixty hours a week and I still can't pay my bills. If I work any harder I won't have a life. I'll just be working, eating and sleeping. Is this just modern life or am I doing something wrong?

Shaolin Master: Make sure that you are devoting your

twenty minutes per day to being alone and quiet. Do this and the answers will begin to come. Are you a careful shopper on a budget? This can save you 10% - 20%. Are you saving 10% - 20% of your income? There is a time value to money. You must save and invest if you hope to end the overwork cycle at some point. In most jobs, 20% of the work yields 80% of the rewards. Are you productive enough to recognize and concentrate on that important 20%? If you work for yourself, this should boost your income. If you work for someone else, this should get you promotions. If you are a hard worker and are not appreciated, you need to find another job. Maybe you need to return to school at night to learn new skills. Your situation is not modern life but all life in all times. Give yourself the gift of quiet time and you will know what to do. Then, do it.

6.
Son is a superior athlete

I think my 10-year-old son is a superior athlete. He is excellent at soccer and basketball and he can hold his own in baseball. Now he wants to add karate to his schedule. Is this a good idea or is he doing too much?

Shaolin Master: A well-rounded child will have time for only one sport, two at the most. How about discussing with him the benefits of spending some extra time reading or on schoolwork? Can you cultivate and encourage an interest in music or art lessons or learning a foreign language? If your son is a superior athlete, would he consider coaching younger children or a child with special needs? If karate isn't his first or second choice, leave it alone for now.

7.
Exercising and not looking so good

I have been faithfully exercising thirty minutes a day as you recommend in the Master Success Course and I feel better, but I don't look any better. I want to look better, so how much more do I have to do?

Shaolin Master: Congratulations on starting and sticking to an exercise plan. If you have thirty minutes, then stretch for five minutes, do aerobic exercise for fifteen, do five minutes of strength work and cool down stretch for five minutes. You will be healthy. If you want to start looking reasonably good, you should extend your program to 45 minutes to an hour. If you want to look like a magazine model, double that time to 90 minutes to two hours per day for five to six days per week. And, of course, watch your diet. It isn't easy. It is possible.

8.
Fear of funerals

My best friend's mother is terminally ill. She is expected to pass away soon and I can't go to funerals. You say that everyone has a fear and this one is mine. How should I handle this with my friend?

Shaolin Master: Obviously, in this period of family sadness, this isn't a good time to talk about your problems. When your friend's mother dies, it won't be a good time either. You owe it to your best friend to pay proper respect. You can send flowers and a sympathy card. If it is viewing the body that you fear, perhaps you can go to the funeral home and sit in the waiting room rather than the viewing room. If there is a wake and a church service, perhaps you can make an excuse and skip the funeral home but go to the church and cemetery. Or, you may decide to face your fear. Take action. Do your best.

9.
A sister's divorce

My sister is going through a very messy and painful divorce. I've run out of advice for her. What do I do now?

Shaolin Master: You say, "I'm sorry." You say, "I'm sorry" and you stay quiet and you listen. That's the best sister that you can be for your sister. Be there and listen. Unless your sister is exhibiting some type of self-destructive behavior, your intervention is probably not warranted and probably not helpful.

10.
Honoring family vacation time

I have three kids who are all involved in various sports, a husband who is a workaholic, and I work part-time. I don't think our schedules will ever coincide enough for us to have very much family time or any vacation time. What's a stressed-out family to do?

Shaolin Master: This takes leadership. So, assume the lead. Schedule planning takes work and discipline. Start with a family meeting and decide on at least one season when all the kids are not playing any sports. Vote. Choose one off-season and stick to your guns. No exceptions. No excuses. Then, mom and dad have to free their weekends and a week or two of family vacation time. No exceptions. No excuses. You want to be a family and not a group of housemates. Agree on family time and then plan lots of family fun activities and trips.

11.
Is walking enough?

Forget the fancy health clubs and treadmills, I believe in walking as exercise. Aren't I right in saying that walking is enough?

Shaolin Master: If you walk thirty to forty-five minutes for five or six days per week, you have an excellent exercise program. Just watch your diet and add a little strength work. Make sure that part of your walk is done at a brisk pace or uphill to get your heart going. To avoid injury, stretch before and after your walk. If you walk alone and without headphones, you'll also gain your quiet time benefits. You may be able to combine fitness training into your work activity schedule by setting 10,000 steps as your daily walking goal. Park the car a few blocks away. Forget the elevator. Get yourself a pedometer and get going.

12.
Women black belts

I am a woman who is interested in studying karate. My concern is getting hurt. Suppose that I study for five years and get a black belt, what are the odds of my not getting injured? Isn't karate pretty dangerous?

Shaolin Master: Karate is a contact sport. As you advance, so does the intensity of contact. Karate is about punching and kicking and takedowns and blocking and sparring. Especially at the brown belt level, the training and competition can be (should be) intense. Muscle sprains and strains are common. Broken fingers and toes (and noses) are not uncommon. Martial arts training is not particularly more dangerous than prolonged expert level competitive training in skiing, gymnastics, rock climbing and bicycling, as well as, tennis, running and even swimming. Sorry, but if you want non-contact, choose tai chi or yoga and not karate. If you find a dojo that will guarantee you a black belt while guaranteeing that you won't feel a scratch, put your hand on your wallet and leave immediately.

13.
A writing career

My dream is to become a journalist. How did you get started writing?

Shaolin Master: I wanted to become a writer and the subject that I knew the most about was real estate. There was a man in Boston, Jack Peckham, who wrote a very popular real estate column every Sunday in the *Boston Herald*. I called him and asked him if I could buy him lunch. I wanted advice. He hired me as a part-time researcher. I worked for Jack for about six years as a ghostwriter before I ever had my name on a column. I continued writing for Jack and was hired as a writer by Federal Research Press. All this time I was still a high school teacher and I was writing about 30 hours a week. But, if you love what you're doing, it doesn't seem like work. I just about equaled my teaching salary as a writer. In the 1980s, there were only about six people who were making a full-time living as real estate writers. This was a very small group. I have always considered myself a teacher and not a writer. For me, writing is a trade.

So, it was all about making that first phone call. Making that call at the right time. Wanting the job enough to start at the bottom. Being good enough at the trade. Paying my dues for a long time before getting my own work. It was a long road but it happened. Start down the road and if you are determined, good luck will walk with you.

14.
Harassed in the park

There is a man who lives by himself in our apartment building. I think he's a little slow. He has some kind of a factory job. He doesn't drive. I feel sorry for him because I've never seen him do much more than sit in the park and feed the pigeons. The other day, I saw this group of boys harassing him. They weren't a gang or anything, just about six boys heading home from school who thought that it would be fun to throw empty peanut shells at this poor man and to call him "bird brain." I was in the park and I didn't do anything and it's been bothering me ever since. I'm a woman in my forties, what should I have done?

Shaolin Master: Mother Teresa, for all the suffering she witnessed, said that the worst disease is loneliness. Be neighborly. Learn this fellow's name. Greet him by name when you see him. Encourage others in your family and building to do likewise. Ask after his well being. Include him in family and building activities when it is appropriate. When you have formed this neighborly bond, you will be much more likely to take the necessary direct action without pause.

"Listening to your instincts" is an important Action Principle. Are these just a few ten-year-old boys "having fun?" Then you can shoo them away with, "All right fellas, that's enough. Get going." And, you can let them know that you know "Bob or Dave" the victim by name. However, if you sense any physical danger, use your cell phone and call 911. This is a police matter and this is what the police are trained and paid to do.

15.
A screaming daughter

Whenever I have an argument with my teenage daughter, she gets right in my face and screams back that if she has problems, I'm to blame for all of them. It's always my fault that she's sloppy and lazy and mean. How can I stop this behavior?

Shaolin Master: Of course, you should apologize for being such a terrible parent and causing her so much anguish. Then suggest that she rebel by being neat and ambitious and kind. Why not ask her how you can be a better parent and raise a better child? What rules should a parent impose to encourage proper behavior? Then allow her to live by her own strict guidelines.

16.
The most dangerous people

I know that you teach self-defense but I'll tell you that I think there's a much greater chance that I'll be killed or injured by a drunk or reckless driver on the street than by a mugger. Do you agree and what can I do?

Shaolin Master: You are absolutely right. Martial arts training teaches one to be alert and aware. These are important skills when walking or driving. There are some bad people walking the streets. There are lots of selfish people driving cars who routinely risk lives by having a few extra drinks or speeding to "important" appointments.

Unfortunately, with selfish people common sense doesn't work. Punishment does work. In Germany, a first offense for drunk driving mandates the loss of your license for a year. The second offense and you can never get a driver's license again. If that were our policy, and that policy were strictly enforced, deaths from drunk driving would plummet. Why don't we do this? Why do we feel sorry for the selfish drunk who drives and endangers all of us? Also, too many selfish drunks who lose their licenses continue to drive. We need to take the licenses and impound the cars for the duration of the license suspension. Let's all speak up!

17.
Too much self-help

I like to read motivational books. I read you and Tony Robbins and Napoleon Hill and Norman Vincent Peale and Deepak Chopra and lots more. I'm just wondering how much of this stuff really works. For example, how many successes do you think you have?

Shaolin Master: Napoleon Hill is the father of American motivational literature. He estimated that between 1% and 3% of readers actually followed his advice. Most diets work if you follow them. Most motivational advice works if you follow the advice. It's easier to dismiss motivational advice as "Oh, yeah, I already knew that," than it is to roll up your sleeves and get to work. This can be your mantra, "Most don't. I will. Most don't. I will." It is true that most don't, but you can. You can do it day-by-day and step-by-step. Now, if Napoleon Hill is in the 1%-3% success range, I must be helping a fraction of a fraction. But, I'm still persistent and I know you are also!

18.
My first karate master

I'm curious to know who was your karate master and how he influenced you. Can you share with us?

Shaolin Master: I have had the privilege of studying with several outstanding Shaolin Kempo Masters and with Grandmaster Fred Villari. My current master is Master Mark Grupposo, an 8th degree black belt from Natick, Massachusetts. My first master was John Fritz. John is now a 9th degree black belt and runs a wellness center in Jupiter, Florida.

John was a genuine leader. There was no phoniness about him. You felt that he genuinely cared about your well-being and progress. He made every student feel like a friend, white belt or black belt. During every visit, at some point, John would stop to say "Hello," to ask what you were working on, and to offer a small bit of advice. His private attention might only take two or three minutes but it made you feel special. I learned a lot of karate, a lot about business and a lot about being a caring person from Master John. I owe him.

19.
Using the term Master

Where does the term "Master" come from? Do you expect people to call you "Master?" Don't you think that this word is pretty awkward as a title?

Shaolin Master: In Shaolin Kempo, a master is a teacher who has achieved the rank of 5th degree black belt or higher. It is a title of respect given to a senior teacher to be used by his or her students in the dojo. Non-students have no need to use the title and students outside the dojo have no obligation to use the title. When we meet, my name is Bill. My favorite name is Uncle Bill to several dozen nieces and nephews and assorted others.

If you follow my teaching, you know that I believe that anyone who follows the Action Principles and tries their best every day to live a life of self-improvement and service to others is a Master. I would certainly not hesitate to bow to such a person to show my respect for their positive commitment to a better world.

20.
Can't afford college

I am a high school sophomore and I study hard and get good grades. I would like to go to a good college but I don't think my parents can afford the tuition for any really good college. I know it's wrong but I feel sorry for myself. Should I talk to my parents? How should I get over this or should I just forget about going to a good college?

Shaolin Master: You're right. Don't feel sorry for yourself. You aren't confined to a hospital bed. You aren't living in a tent in a refugee camp. You haven't been drafted to go to war. Re-read your Action Principles and start being a lot more self-reliant. Thank your parents for getting you this far and certainly don't blame them for your lack of funding. What does a "good college" even mean? Take an interest in your studies. Ask questions. Get your assignments done. Read and keep reading. Ultimately, your choice of a college matters much less than your attitude as a student. All education is ultimately self-education.

You can go to college and work part-time. You can go to a co-op college where you work one semester and study another. You can go to a less expensive state college. You can join the National Guard and earn tuition monies while serving your country on weekends. You can get loans. Where there is a will, there are lots of ways. Find one or find two.

I know I probably sound like an old man (I'm only in my fifties), but I went to a state college and worked 30-40 hours a week and I served in the Army Reserve – all at the same time. You can too.

21.
Finding good help

I manage a supermarket and my biggest problem is finding and retaining good help. It seems like nobody wants to work very hard any more and trying to get employees to be customer service oriented is impossible. I observed one young employee rudely answering a customer's question and when I confronted her she said, "Listen, back off. This is the way I am. If you want to fire me, fire me. I can get $12-an-hour jobs every day of the week." What can I do?

Shaolin Master: Certainly give this young woman the opportunity to prove her assertion and find work elsewhere. At least this woman will serve as an example to your other employees that rudeness will not be tolerated. Plainly and simply, employees must understand that it is the customers who spend the money so that the company can have the profits to pay their salaries. It is the customer's money that ultimately becomes their money. Customers who are treated rudely will exercise their options to shop somewhere else. This is simple: no customers, no business.

Everything starts with your leadership to be hard working and pleasant and encouraging. Schedule weekly meetings where you can share customer service ideas and listen to customer horror stories. The best way to retain good employees is to provide a superior working environment. Make sure that your best employees know that you acknowledge and appreciate their work. The best way to find good employees is to start a referral network where your employees become your recruiters looking for new co-workers. You might offer a bonus for finding a new hire and then a second bonus if that new employee stays with the company for six months.

22.
Feelings of failure

I am 65 years old and often I get depressed thinking that I didn't do enough with my life. I am haunted by "should have dones." Will any of your courses or materials help me feel better about myself?

Shaolin Master: I can only encourage. You must act. Here are three letters that I want you to remember "NDY" which stand for "Not Dead Yet!" Get up early tomorrow morning and see the sunrise. Talk a walk and look at the wonders of life. You are alive. Make sure that you are investing 20 minutes a day in quiet time and the answers will come. You must keep learning. Read books. Watch the news. Sign up for an adult ed course. You must get involved. Stop feeling sorry for yourself. There are many local organizations that need you as a volunteer. There are many lonely people who need your companionship. You will feel loved. You will feel respected. You need exciting plans. How about planning a trip to London, Paris or Hong Kong? With the right attitude, you will find all of my books and courses interesting and helpful. Without the right attitude, books and courses are a waste of money. Please, at my age, 65 doesn't sound old.

23.
Martial arts schools and styles

I want to start martial arts training and I can't find anyone who teaches Shaolin Kempo in my area. What is the next best style of the martial arts?

Shaolin Master: Do not be so concerned about style. In the first years of training, all styles are more or less the same. In your latter years of training, all styles are more or less the same. Find a master or sensei that you like and a dojo with a class schedule that suits your schedule. Don't sign any long contracts. Ask if you can view and/or participate in a few sample classes. Is the focus on competition or conditioning or general learning? What do your instincts tell you about the teaching atmosphere? If you don't feel comfortable, you won't stick with a program.

24.
No pet policies

I know that you were in real estate and will probably defend landlords, but I think it's terrible that so few apartment complexes allow pets. I'd like to get a dog. I think that I have a right to have a pet if I want one but I can't find an apartment that will take a dog. Why are landlords so mean when it comes to pets, especially dogs?

Shaolin Master: If everyone were a responsible pet owner, there would be fewer "no pet" policies, but unfortunately this is not the case. The little old lady with the toy poodle is not the problem. The problem is the young guy down the hall who sees the old lady with the poodle and decides that two rotweillers would be cool. However, when the young guy gets the rotweillers, he quickly finds out how much work they can be, and the dogs start to become a problem for everyone in the building. This is just a story to illustrate a point. It is not about breeds of dogs and the ages of pet owners. It is about responsible and irresponsible pet owners. One irresponsible pet owner can have a detrimental effect on the peace and wellbeing of many tenants.

Owning rental apartments is a business. If an owner can find tenants without pets to fill his units, you will see "no pet" policies. If you are in a high vacancy area, you will see "pet friendly" policies. The best solution to your situation is to work hard, save and buy your own house.

25.
No kill policies

I know that the US has a "no kill" policy against assassinating foreign leaders, but is it morally right for us to do nothing if a foreign leader decides to commit genocide against his own people?

Shaolin Master: There is evil in the world. There are individuals who will kill all in their path in a lust for power. Under the auspices of the War Crimes Tribunal or the United Nations, we should act swiftly in the face of genocide. We have Special Forces troops who understand the risks of combat and yet are ready, willing and able to take direct action. Instead, we seem to prefer a cowardly approach of bombing

from five miles high, when all we succeed in doing is killing innocent civilians. The despot lives on to propagandize his people against us and create more mayhem. We don't need a "no kill" policy. We need a "Let's apprehend quickly" policy. There are very few Hitlers and Stalins and Pol Pots, but they do exist. We need the will to act.

24

26.
Black belt with a gun

A friend of mine belongs to a karate club and he tells me that some of the black belts carry guns. To me, this is preposterous. Why would you study karate if you were just going to carry a gun anyway?

Shaolin Master: The martial arts are warrior arts. Most systems, especially in the upper ranks, train with weapons. To be a warrior, you train with ancient farming tools such as tonfas, nunchaku and kamas. To be a modern warrior, you can train with knives, mace and firearms. The skill of the martial artist comes in knowing when to fight and then, without hesitation, fighting to win with all weapons available. The skill of the martial artist comes in knowing when to bow quietly and walk away. Whether ones defends with punches or bullets is irrelevant.

27.
Prosperity before peace

I am somewhat interested in your self-help ideas but I really need a system that is going to make me serious money. I want to be a peaceful person, but making money has got to come first if I want a family and house and car and other good things. What are your guarantees?

Shaolin Master: I guarantee you hard work. I guarantee you'll make foolish mistakes. I guarantee you'll need to learn self-denial. I guarantee you'll have to simplify your life.

In exchange for being a faithful follower of the Action Principles, I believe that after 6 years, you will no longer be particularly consumed by making money and after 20 years, your investment will have grown to the point that you can switch to part-time work or even retire young.

Every day you will be working to be the best employer or employee that you can be. Every day you will be focused on the needs of those you work for and those who work for you. You will be liked. You will be admired. You will be trusted. You will be the person who gets promoted. You will be the person with a backlog of customers. You will be successful. You will be prosperous. But, it all begins with your believing in the power of the Action Principles to help you be the best you.

28.
Martial arts at 68

I am 68 years old and I love the Action Principles and I'm doing my quiet time every day. Since I'm about to retire, I've been using my quiet time to consider my options. I'm a Korean War veteran and while I was in the service I taught hand-to-hand combat. That was a long time ago. I remember thinking about earning my black belt, but career and family and all the usual stuff got in the way. And, back in the '50s, there weren't very many martial arts schools around. I'm thinking about going to a dojo to inquire about lessons. You can be honest. How crazy an idea is this?

Shaolin Master: I think it's a great idea. Don't hesitate. I certainly am going to continue studying, practicing and teaching to your age and as far beyond as God permits. You might have to go to a few different dojos but I don't feel that you are really going to have trouble finding a group that will welcome you. With your doctor's permission, go for the black belt. In Asia, it is common to see older folks in the parks in the mornings doing their Tai Chi exercises. I'm not ashamed to be seen if you aren't. Go for it and have fun. I know you will.

29.
Traditional karate versus kempo karate

What is the difference between traditional karate and kempo karate?

Shaolin Master: There are many styles of karate from traditional to eclectic. Traditional karate styles would emphasize very specific forms and punches and kicks. A traditional instructor would be quite strict in defining the right way and the wrong way to do things. Kempo is much more wide open and forgiving. In kempo, the motto is "if it works, use it." Kempo is hard and direct and immediate. It is hitting someone over the head with a chair if hitting someone over the head with a chair is the best self-defense tool available. A traditionalist isn't likely to be practicing techniques with a rock or pen or rolled-up magazine. A kempo stylist would say, "Why not?" In all styles, it is speed, surprise and aggression that quickly overwhelms and wins confrontations.

30.
Nervous about a job change

I own a sub shop and take home about $600 a week. That's not a bad living, but I want more for my family and myself. I'm thinking about selling the shop and going into the real estate business. Of course, I've been thinking about doing this for five years. How can I get over my nerves?

Shaolin Master: I hope you are spending your twenty minutes per day in quiet time. This is the time when the ideas and answers will come. You may already have your answer,  which is to not make the move from food to property. Remember, just because you are knowledgeable and successful in one field does not mean that you can automatically switch your talents to a completely different field.

Start from a strong base that for you is your sub shop. In this field, you are an expert, and your expertise gives you a competitive edge. Can you expand the menu? Can you open a second new shop? Can you expand by buying another existing shop? Can you add more seats? Can you find any wholesale opportunities for your subs or other items? Always study your industry leaders. Find the shops that are netting $800, $1,000, and $1,500 per week and figure out why. Copy success.

Then, you can take your extra profits and make solid safe real estate investments. You will win-win.

31.
A gun seen at school

Last night, my son told me that last week he saw one of his classmates showing a gun that he had hidden in a gym bag to another boy. My son was afraid to say anything until now. I guess this incident has blown over but what could my son have done without getting involved? He says now that he doesn't know if the gun was real.

Shaolin Master: Your son should have reported this matter immediately to a teacher that he trusts. Most schools now have a "zero weapons tolerance policy" and established guidelines for dealing with such inappropriate behavior. It is the job of trained school personnel to confront the offender and determine the seriousness of the situation and the proper response. At the very least, the offender has exercised poor judgment and should be counseled. Again, make sure that your son has a teacher that he can go to in an emergency.

32.
Mom in a nursing home

I feel like a prisoner. My husband and I have lived in my mother's house for the past twenty-five years. My mother is elderly and she has started to do bizarre things like leaving the stove on when she has nothing to cook and unplugging our refrigerator to save us money. My husband and I are at our wit's end. My problem is my brother. I know that if we put my mother into a nursing home, he is going to insist that we sell the house and give him half the money. Now, my brother has done nothing for my mother and doesn't deserve the house. Should I get a lawyer or what should I do?

Shaolin Master: Before getting a lawyer, I think your first obligation is to get a doctor to properly diagnose your mother's condition. Perhaps she can be helped at home. Perhaps she would benefit from some form of assisted living. When an appropriate treatment plan has been written, then, depending upon her Social Security, her other assets and other insurance, you can design a program to pay for that treatment. There are professionals who specialize in these matters and they can advise you as to the applicable laws. The needs of your mother must come first.

If your mother is deemed mentally competent, then she can decide if she wants to sell her house to you and, if so, what share if any should go to your brother. It is her house and her decision. If your mother is not mentally competent, then you need a lawyer or the courts to arbitrate a settlement with your brother. He will get something regardless of your personal relationship with him or your opinion of him.

33.
Son looking at porn

I went on the Internet the other night and was completely shocked to find that a porn site had been bookmarked. The culprit can only be my 14-year old son. I am devastated. We are a good Christian family. My son obviously needs counsel-

ing. My husband is no help and says that looking at porn at my son's age is normal but I want it to stop. What should I say to my son and husband and what type of counseling do you think my son needs?

Shaolin Master: You should tell your husband and son that you love them. Curiosity about the opposite sex and sex in general is perfectly normal in a boy your son's age. In fact, a lack of interest would be abnormal. If the porn is of a deviant nature or if the situation changes from being of casual interest to being a consuming interest, then there is a problem that requires professional counseling.

34.
A rich kid writes

I'm twenty-six years old and very successful for my age. I do live at home but I have a nice fat bank account. In general, I like the advice you give, so I would like your opinion. I have my eye on a new sports car (price tag – over $35K). I know that you say that people who work hard should spoil themselves, so I think that I'm entitled to this little indulgence. My problem is that I don't want to make my friends feel bad since they don't make as much as I do and could never afford a car like this. Should I go ahead and get the car anyway?

Shaolin Master: First, I'd like to commend you on your success. Then, I'd like to sit down with you and find out why you would so foolishly squander your blessings and talents.

I think that buying that sports car would be a mistake. Why

not buy a nice car for $15K and use the other $20K plus interest that you don't spend on the car to buy a piece of property and move out of your parents' house? In twenty years, that old sports car will have been crushed and turned into a lamp base. In twenty years, that home investment could be worth hundreds of thousands of dollars in equity.

You think that your new car will impress your friends but it will probably have the opposite effect. You may be seen as an arrogant show-off and resented.

35.
Dalai Lama, Pope and Shaolin Master

I am still unclear as to what a Shaolin Master is. Is the Shaolin Master like the Dalai Lama or the Pope?

Shaolin Master: A Shaolin Master is a senior martial arts instructor. He or she is not a religious figure any more than a basketball coach or baseball manager. Coaches, managers and Shaolin Masters teach. As teachers, they may or may not have something relevant to say. They may or may not be good motivators. This is for you to decide. You must choose your own teachers. When the student is ready, the teacher arrives.

I seriously doubt that the Dalai Lama or the Pope would ever answer a question by saying that an appropriate response to a situation would be to hit someone over the head with a chair. I might.

36.
Will the real Shaolin Master stand up?

How do I know that you are the "real" Shaolin Master? I have seen lots of other people in the martial arts claim to be Shaolin Masters.

Shaolin Master: This is a very important distinction. I am not "the" Shaolin Master. I am Bill FitzPatrick, "a" Shaolin Master. At one time, the Villari organization in which I study had over 300 schools. Almost 10,000 students have been promoted to black belts over a thirty-year period. Of this number, Grandmaster Villari has promoted about 50 people to the rank of 5th degree or above, making each of them Shaolin Masters. Just in the U.S., there are many other styles besides Villari that use the name "Shaolin" and, obviously, in China and throughout Asia, there are many "Shaolin Masters." I am far from unique as a Shaolin Master.

37.
Completely stressed out

I know about your saying that people should take twenty minutes a day to meditate but I haven't got five minutes to myself. I have three school age kids. I have a job. I have a husband. Explain to me how I can find time for myself.

Shaolin Master: Welcome to modern life. You above all

people should be taking some quiet time for yourself. It can be done. You need a prioritized to-do list. Try to finish or make progress on the top three items on your list. Then, at the end of the day, you can be thankful that you have accomplished some important things and done your best.

Be thankful for your children. Be thankful for your job. Be thankful for your husband. Everyone doesn't have the blessing that you have. If you absolutely, positively can't find the time during the day, then get up a little earlier or stay up a little later. It will be a sacrifice, but worth the effort.

38.
Black belts are cheap

I have a friend who is a martial artist; in fact, he's a black belt. But he hasn't trained in five years because he is disgusted at how low the standards have dropped. He says that now-a-days karate schools are just about selling black belts. I'm still impressed when someone says that they are a black belt, but should I be?

Shaolin Master: Anyone can go into any martial arts store and buy a black belt. You won't be asked to perform any techniques or katas. You won't have to show a testing certificate. A black belt should only cost you three or four dollars. If all someone was interested in was the belt, this is the way to go. Why spend thousands of dollars and years of your life training?

Is there a difference in standards? Of course, there is. You can go to an Ivy League college and get a great education. You can go to a state college and get a great education. You can go to an Ivy League college or a state college and graduate an ignorant buffoon. Ultimately, all education and training is self-education and self-training. Are you working to do your best, or are you simply cruising, hoping to squeak by on the next test?

Thankfully, I think that the black belts that you have met are real black belts. You can see it in their presence, in their confidence. Phonies are usually pretty easy to spot. Encourage your friend to return to teaching and set appropriately high standards.

39.
I liked the old success.org

I like the old success.org better than this new dojo.com website. I'm really not into all this karate stuff and there is too much of it. Why did you make the change?

Shaolin Master: One of the fundamentals of leadership is that people follow people and not movements. I had been trying my best to promote the Action Principles. We had reached a worldwide distribution of over 100,000 copies in print (and many more e-copies) but I felt the movement had stalled. I think one reason is that the Action Principles lack the strong credibility of authorship. In other words, who was writing these principles and why should I care?

In business, it is important to have a UVP or Unique Value

Perspective. Among motivational writers, my UVP is as the Shaolin Master. I write, conduct seminars and make personal appearances as the Shaolin Master. The word "dojo" is one of the most recognizable words in the martial arts. As I establish my connection to the Action Principles, it makes sense to use the strongest URL owned by the American Success Institute, which is dojo.com.

I hope that you will give us a chance to prove ourselves at dojo.com. Our plans include exciting innovations. Our mission to help you be your best remains the same.

40.
Asian travels plans

I attended both nights of your seminar in Singapore and was really quite motivated. When are you coming back?

Shaolin Master: We have established a working partnership with the Master Trainer Institute (New York and Singapore) under the leadership of Dr. Mel Gill. It was Dr. Mel who sponsored my visit to Singapore. I hope to return to Southeast Asia in 2002 for a longer stay. As you would know, the people of Singapore were welcoming and friendly. Your country is a natural beauty. My visit to your Botanical Gardens (and the Long Bar at Raffles!) is etched in my memory. I thank you. If you enjoyed the seminar, please call Mel and let him know.

41.
Pushing real estate

Your advice seems to push people toward buying real estate as an investment. This may be for some people, but I haven't got the time to manage property and I can't stand the idea of being a landlord. Why the pressure?

Shaolin Master: More money has been made in real estate than in all other investments combined. Making a decision to buy is really making a decision to secure your housing future and not to pay rent to someone else. If you have the choice, why should you be subject to another's rules and regulations and rent increases? Buy your own home. You don't have to become a landlord to enjoy the principal benefits of real estate investing. Now, about that summerhouse …

42.
Become a world authority

I've always had an interest in eastern philosophy similar to the base from which you write your ideas. My dream job would be to teach at a university. My problem is that I'm in my late forties and I don't have any formal training in philosophy. My bachelor's degree is in economics. Do you think it's too late for me to consider this as a realistic second career?

Shaolin Master: Of course not, go for it. It is said that you can be considered an expert on a subject by reading twelve books and a world authority by reading forty-eight books.

Who's stopping you but yourself? Yes, if you have to work full time, getting a Master's Degree might take you five years and a Doctorate another seven years, but who's stopping you but yourself? In a few years, you may be able to start teaching part-time at an adult education center or community college level. Then, build your second career from there. Let your love of philosophy fill you with enthusiasm and you'll be a great teacher.

43.
The problem with immigrants

Immigrants are a problem. They come to this country and take away our jobs. They are here for only a few years and they're already buying houses and starting businesses. How can this country stay strong if we allow this influx to continue?

Shaolin Master: How can this country stay strong without the people you are talking about? And, I honestly don't know what country you're from. You could be from Berlin or New York or Singapore or Florence or Casablanca or London or Paris or Prague or Moscow or Tokyo. I've heard this same lament in all these places.

Why take this narrow perspective? Do you have a house? Do you have a job? Do you have a business? Who is stopping you? If you were a hard working person with a positive attitude and the right accent, I'd say your odds of being hired are much better than a lazy person with a negative attitude with an unusual accent. Worry about yourself and your family. If you see people working hard and buying property, here is my advice – copy them!

44.
Too fat to fight

It's not nice to say but some of the policeman and fireman in our city are grossly overweight and certainly not role models for our children. I've even seen some police officers walking down the street with cigarettes dangling from their lips. Where are the standards? If there were trouble, some of these people couldn't huff and puff fast enough to get out of their own way. I own a local business and I can't afford to alienate these people. Can anything be done?

Shaolin Master: You are doing it. You are speaking up. And, you are bringing up a legitimate and potentially serious problem. As a citizen and taxpayer, you pay for protection for your life and property and you deserve the best protection that your money can buy. However, a frontal attack might not work, since these problem officers could probably claim civil rights violations or union protections. Take an opposite, more subtle approach by praising the fitness and readiness of the officers with enough pride in their jobs to stay in shape. Find the role models on the forces and tell the chiefs of police and fire and your local officials how much you admire these exemplary men and women. Keep it up. Encourage your fellow citizens to do the same and the word will get out and back to the slackers. Of course, without pride, anyone in any line of work probably has personal problems beyond their employment and will not be receptive to constructive criticism. You can hope that new recruits will be contracted under a different higher standard and held to that standard.

45.
Caught shoplifting

I caught my eleven-year-old daughter shoplifting. She had two new rings that I know she didn't buy and she admitted taking them. I brought the rings back to the store but at the store, they had all these signs posted about prosecuting shoplifters. I panicked and left. I still have the rings. What should I do with them? And, I want to speak to my daughter but I don't want to make a big deal out of it because as she told me "all the kids" do it and why should she be prosecuted and have her life ruined over two small dumb rings?

Shaolin Master: The rings are easy. Put them in an envelope and mail them to the store manager with the simple words "found in the parking lot." You don't have to explain further or give names.

"All the kids" do not shoplift. Shoplifting is stealing. Whether the theft is two rings or two hundred diamond rings is irrelevant. Your daughter must realize that if she had been caught by store security, her future could have been compromised. This would be an extremely serious consequence. Most importantly, she must realize that stealing from others diminishes her as a person. If she wants to be her best, this isn't it.

You must decide on an appropriate punishment and then stick to it. Your daughter must be disciplined if she is to have a happy life.

46.

Concentrate on your customers

I'd like to open my own real estate office but there are already four offices in my town. I don't know if there is enough real estate activity to support a fifth business. In favor of the idea, I can say that I'm a hard worker and have lots of contacts. Should I give it a try or forget it?

Shaolin Master: Let's say that you open an office that is the fifth in town and there is only enough business for four offices, who is to say that your office will be the one not to survive? If you offer a quality service, if you work hard, if you concentrate on customer service, the other four should be the ones to worry. Another approach might be to find a niche market. Perhaps you can specialize in investment real estate or land or commercial property or industrial buildings. Study your market and concentrate on your customers. If you have the will, you will find a way.

47.

Retire early

I'm thirty-five and my goal in life is to retire at sixty. I want to be sitting on a beach with a laptop writing mystery novels. My problem is that I have zero saved for retirement. How can I get myself back on track and into a savings habit?

Shaolin Master: If you have zero saved, you aren't getting back on track, because you've never been on track. Just like everyone else, if you want to be a saver, you need discipline. If you want to retire in twenty years, you'll need to immediately save and invest twenty percent of your income. If you don't own a home, my first goal would be to buy a house or condo with a twenty-year mortgage. Then, I would follow the real estate investment program outlined in the Master Success Course. If you don't like real estate, then you should consider a broad based mutual fund specializing in long-term growth.

You have outlined a good challenge for yourself. It won't be easy but it will be possible. Remember, if you become a knowledgeable consumer and work from a written household budget, that alone will save you 10%- 15%. The rest will come from some overtime and promotions. Most people could not do what you are proposing, but you can.

48.
Too politically correct

I am a seventeen-year-old African-American woman. Next year I'll be a senior and the Captain of the Academic Decathlon at my high school. This means that I get to pick the seven other students on my team that will represent our school. Because we are an inner city school, my faculty advisor is strongly hinting that at least half of my picks should be minority students. I resent this and I think it's racist. I think that I should be able to pick the best students regardless of race. Am I right?

Shaolin Master: As Captain, the best thing that you can do for your school is to assemble the best possible team with the greatest chance of winning. Is the football coach or the basketball coach being asked to be politically correct? We must all work together to eliminate barriers that can separate us. Excellence is excellence and is not subject to conditions of race, color, creed, national origin, etc. Speaking up may take some courage, but you can do what is right. Good luck with your competition and your team will be lucky to have you as Captain.

49.
A gossip at work

I know that I have a serious problem with gossiping. I know that gossiping is negative. I want to be more positive. My big problem comes at lunchtime when all us girls sit around and talk about everyone else and everything that's happening. Honestly, I like it. How can I break this negative habit?

Shaolin Master: Don't judge yourself too harshly too quickly. Is what you are doing gossiping or normal conversation? It's interesting to hear about someone's kids and to offer opinions. It is interesting to speculate on the opposite sex. It is interesting to talk about clothes and hairstyles and vacations and TV shows and even office romances. The question is whether the talk is fun spirited or mean spirited. You know the difference.

For argument's sake, let's say that the talk is mostly negative and you feel a need to take a break. Do just that. Don't make a big deal about it. Don't over explain. Tell the gang that you are on a new health regime and take a walk for twenty minutes. This can be your quiet time. Or, you can walk for five minutes and sit down with a book for ten minutes and then walk back. This is a constructive use of your time. You break habits or gain habits one step at a time. Remember, the only people who don't talk about other people are those on ego trips.

50.
Cardio-kickboxing

I've been taking cardio-kickboxing lessons for the past two months. I've lost six pounds and I'm having a ball. What is your opinion on cardio-kickboxing as a martial art?

Shaolin Master: I'm glad you're enjoying the wonderful aerobic health benefits of cardio-kickboxing lessons. You're proving that's its both a great way to lose weight and to have fun. However, cardio-kickboxing is to the martial arts what playing the air guitar is to actually playing the guitar. The kicks and punches are only simulations of the real thing. It may look like the real thing but it isn't. Cardio-kickboxing is not a martial art.

51.
A put-down artist

Like a good daughter, I go to my parents' house every Sunday for dinner. But, it isn't easy. My mother is the Queen of Put-Down Artists. She criticizes everything about me. It's my weight. It's my hair. It's my boyfriends. It's my smoking. Should I stop going? Is there anything I can say to her?

Shaolin Master: You can't change your mother. You can make your position clear and hope that your mother changes. You can say, "Mom, I love you but your comments are hurting me." When it happens again, you have to say, "Mom, I know you love me but your comments are hurting me." You can say, "Mom your comments are hurting me and rather than stay for four hours on Sunday I'm only going to stay for one hour or I'm only going to come every other Sunday." However, I presume that if you are following the Action Principles that you are trying to make improvements in your life. So, maybe you can say, "Mom, I'm so lucky to have you. My smoking is down to ten cigarettes a day and I'm having salads three days a week for lunch. Mom, thanks for the encouragement. Now, let's talk about someone or something else."

52.
An obnoxious tenant

I just bought a four-family house and one of the tenants has got to go. I don't care that he's lived in the building for thirty years. He is still a pain in the neck and my "you know what." I told him about a modest rent increase and he started to tell me everything wrong with the building. I don't need to hear this. I need good tenants who pay the rent and don't complain. Wouldn't you kick him out? Tell me I'm wrong.

Shaolin Master: You're wrong. One of the most valuable lessons that I ever learned in real estate investing was to "love your tenants." You borrow hundreds of thousands of dollars to make your investment and to secure your future and your tenants pay this money back for you. God bless them. Love them. In the last thirty years, this "problem" tenant has probably paid for the building several times over with just his rent. Now, he's willing to pay for the building again for you. He probably does know more about your building than any other person. Listen to him. You do need to hear this!

53.
Who is God

I am not a feminist but I do resent the constant portrayal of God as an almighty father. Why can't God be an almighty woman or just an almighty spirit?

Shaolin Master: See God as an almighty mother, father, and brother, sister. See God as a sunrise. See God as a wonderful bite of food. See God as a smile. See God as a kind gesture. See God as all that is good and beautiful. This is the power of your humanness. You can choose.

54.
Lord give me the power to accept

I don't think that I'm a very accepting person. Every day, rude clerks and rude drivers and loud children upset me. Why are we such patsies? Why are we all willing to put up with so much?

Shaolin Master: When you accept that life can be difficult, you won't be surprised when it is. When you accept that you can fail, you can begin and begin again. When you can accept all as your equal, you can rest. When you accept that you will die, you can live. With the good and the bad, we are all in this together. Be the example. Give yourself the gift of twenty minutes each day to celebrate the blessings in your life. Breathe deeply.

55.
He hates ties

I know that this sounds like a nutty question but I'm a high school student and I'm interested in a career in business. My problem is that I hate to wear ties. I also hate to wear suits. I like to be comfortable. There are a lot of pictures of you on the website and you aren't wearing a tie in any of them. Do you agree with me or am I really stupid?

Shaolin Master: I guess I'm more like you. We are alive. We have free will. We can decide to not wear ties. However, I think that the choices you and I make are more than about ties.

If you or I decided to work in a bank or to be stockbrokers, we'd have to wear ties every day. If we were in the Army or worked for McDonalds, we'd have to wear uniforms. We'd have no choice. But, we could be corporate lawyers and need a tie or entertainment lawyers and never need a tie. Or, we could own an advertising agency and insist on informal wear for everyone. We'd be the bosses.

When I teach a karate class, I am expected to wear a karate gi. When I teach a seminar, I am expected to wear a tai chi jacket. The point is that you and I are independent souls who choose to dress comfortably. This is, of course, unless my wife tells me or your parents tell you otherwise.

56.
Training outside the dojo

I've been studying karate for four years and I'm a brown belt. All of my instruction has been inside the dojo, never out. I kind of figure "how realistic can this be?" I think I have good teachers but I'm not so sure. What do you think?

Shaolin Master: Be a leader. Take the initiative. Talk to your instructors. Why not go to the beach, the forest, the parking lot and the office? Why not go out into the rain and snow and scorching heat? Why not wear shorts and then two sweaters and gloves and a jacket. Find out which of your techniques work best in different environments and under different fighting conditions. I'm with you. You've got to vary your training. Get out.

That's what I want to say but it's not my position to second-guess your instructors. Certainly, as a brown belt, you don't want to create too many waves and rock your own boat. Do what you're told. When you become a black belt and have your own students, start offering some more realistic training and I bet your classes will be filled with liked minded souls.

57.
What is enlightenment?

I hear a lot of Buddhist people talking about achieving enlightenment. What does this mean and do you believe in it?

Shaolin Master: Being a Christian, I have neither the training nor authority to explain Buddhism. However, here is my understanding. Enlightenment is a state of bliss in which all becomes clear. You are able to look at life and say, "Aha, I get it now."

To me, enlightenment is not something you achieve but rather a state of realization. You realize that if you improve yourself and help others, you will be happy. To improve yourself, you realize that education and training put you on a lifelong journey. To feel the warmth of respect and love, you realize that others must voluntarily bestow these gifts upon you. Enlightenment is not the end but rather shows you the way to live happily.

58.
Does karate really work?

I've seen a lot of boxing and ultimate fighting and karate kickboxing on TV and everyone seems to survive the bouts.

What gives? If karate really works why isn't everyone dead?

Shaolin Master: Take off the gloves and eliminate all the rules and people would be dead. If you allowed biting and gouging and choking and stomping, people would be dead. Study the rules of ultimate fighting and find out what you aren't allowed to do and you will have your killing techniques. You will learn what the military teaches to their soldiers who might actually have to kill or be killed.

If a two-year-old child accidentally picks up a pen and shoves it into your eye, you will be blind. If a piano accidentally falls on your head, you will be crushed. If a little old lady accidentally runs over you while you are crossing the street, you will be dead. We are all human. We are all subject to the laws of physics. You can't fly. You can't hold your breath under water for ten minutes. If you are hit in the nose by one good punch, the bone will break and your eyes will water and you will lose consciousness. This stuff is real. Be careful and don't forget it.

59.
Vegetarians are best

I feel very strongly that killing animals for food is gross. There are plenty of ways to get good nutrition without the need for eating meat. Most of my girlfriends feel the same way. We are vegetarians. You must be a vegetarian. As high school students, how can we support our cause and get more people involved and save more animals' lives?

Shaolin Master: You sound passionate. Do what you're doing. Write letters and email and speak up. Join groups and form groups. Start debates. Stay informed and always keep reading and researching. Look for new arguments to bolster your position and add to your legitimacy. Find the leaders for your cause, support their efforts and assume a leadership role yourself.

Also, don't be afraid to listen to opposing viewpoints. You aren't learning while you're talking. I am not a vegetarian, but I understand and appreciate your viewpoint. I want to eat less red meat and more leafy vegetables. Maybe, I'm just old fashioned. Now, convince me.

60.
An investment too far

I recently inherited a three-family house. That's the good news. The bad news is that the house is fifty miles from my home. Obviously, I can't travel half a day to fix a leaky faucet. Should I sell or should I hire a local manager or what?

Shaolin Master: Managing one small property from afar is difficult. You could hire a local manager/handyman. Of course, I like the idea of real estate investing. Have you explored real estate investing options closer to home and by that I mean within a ten to fifteen minute drive from home? That move would be worth serious consideration. You might even be able to structure a tax-deferred exchange.

You should have your three-family appraised. You should

find an experienced broker/adviser in your immediate area who specializes in investment real estate. You should speak with an accountant and with an attorney specializing in real estate. Take your time and get the facts. You owe it to yourself, your family and to the person kind enough to remember you in his/her will to maximize the potential of this opportunity.

61.
My Scrapbooks

I saw a picture of you and it looked like you were carrying some sort of scrapbook. Am I being too nosy if I ask what that was?

Shaolin Master: That scrapbook is my organizing system. Each day I update and print my prioritized todo list. I tape the todo list into my spiral notebook. When I take notes during

the day, I use the notebook. When I see an ad I like or I get a businesscard from someone, I tape these in the book. If I'm out walking, I usually have an index card and pen with me and when I get back to the office, the index card is taped in the book. I have a Palm Pilot and several computer organizing systems but my scrapbook is the system that seems to work best for me. I know that I have or don't have everything in one place.

62.
What about religion?

You say that the Shaolin Master isn't religious but you keep talking about religion. What gives?

Shaolin Master: The philosophy underlying the Action Principles is very basic: improve yourself and help others. When you commit yourself to self-improvement and service, you will be happy. All major religions encourage followers to be their best and to "do unto others." It would be impossible to separate these "religious" ideas on happiness from the Action Principles. I am not talking about religion. I am not not talking about religion.

63.
It's in the past

I don't get any credit for any success I have and I resent it. Most people think that I've had it pretty easy because my family had some money, but my father was hardly ever home and my mother was an alcoholic. How can I get over these feelings and what should I say to people?

Shaolin Master: You can't change others' feelings. There is really nothing to say that doesn't make you seem weak. You can only change your own reactions. Because you grew up in a nice house, there are going to be some ignorant or jealous individuals who will see you as spoiled and privileged. People who form opinions without facts are dumb.

This is their problem. It is not your problem unless you dwell on it. Who has a perfect life? Growing up everyone has to deal to some degree with fears, phobias, traumas and parental inadequacies. This is life. This will teach you to be a stronger and more understanding person yourself. Accept this and move on. The past is over. Be thankful that you were able to grow up successfully in spite of your hardships.

64.
Let go and breathe

Is there such a thing as being a nervous person? I always seem to be worried about one small thing after another. Because I'm always fidgeting, the people at work call me "neurotic." I don't want to be like this. I have a good life. What should I do?

Shaolin Master: Let go and breathe. Don't worry about being perfect. Don't worry about getting everything done. Your fidgeting and general nervousness are bad habits that you have to start to correct just like all bad habits. Take your twenty minutes a day to quietly reflect.

Your family is important. Your health is important. Your spirituality is important. Putting toner in the copier, whether you have peas or carrots for dinner, or whether your handbag matches your shoes are not as important. Don't fuel your nervousness by talking about it with others. Deal with it slowly and day by day. Whenever you feel anxious, stop and watch your breath. Breathe in and breathe out. Have a prioritized todo list. Do your best. Your best is good enough. Relax for ten minutes. Relax for twenty minutes. Relax for an hour. Conduct your business in a relaxed manner.

65.
The teachers are terrible

My son really got the short end of the stick this year at his middle school. The poor kid has ended up with what I consider the worst teachers in the building. My son is horrified that I plan to go to the school and insist that he be rescheduled with the good teachers. I don't want to upset my son but I don't want him to lose a year of schooling either. How should I handle this?

Shaolin Master: Without being a part of the school's administration, do you think that you can fairly judge the teaching staff? Where is your information coming from and what might be the agenda of the people rendering opinions? Yes, if you have concerns, you can quietly go to the principal or assistant principal and ask questions without being accusatory or alarming your son. The teachers are guiding your son. You can monitor this guidance at home. You can help with schoolwork and homework. You can encourage reading. You can help your son to love many things and appreciate learning. If you do your part well, your son will turn out fine.

66.
I dreamt that I lived

I want to believe in an afterlife but I'm having a tough time. It just seems to make more sense to believe that you live and die and are gone than it is to believe that you live and die and then go to heaven or hell. Where is heaven and hell? They aren't real places. And, if there isn't a heaven or hell, what's the use of being good or bad?

Shaolin Master: You and I aren't smart enough to answer your question. This is why we have faith in God to help us. We people of Earth know so little. There are thousands of galaxies and millions of planets. How do we know what is intelligent life and what is heaven and hell? Look back a millennium at what people believed. Look forward a millennium to the knowledge to be gained.

You sleep and wake up and your dreams seemed so real. You live your life and you die and you wake up and your life seemed so real. You see good and evil in this life so that you can appreciate heaven in the next. Remember these age-old questions. Do you want to live your life as if there is a God and then find out there isn't? Or, do you want to live your life as if there is no God and then find out there is?

67.
My old man wants a job

I don't know how to handle my father. He is 74 and a

retired lawyer. Our town has a wonderful senior center but he refuses to go. Instead, he has applied to be a bag boy at our local supermarket. I think he's crazy even considering such a job. If he feels the need to work, let him go back to his work – law. Anyway, he doesn't need the money. How can I drum some sense into him?

Shaolin Master: I don't see the problem. And, I don't think that your father's decision is about money. He wants to be active. He wants to be active in his own way. He wants to meet lots of people of all ages and chat. Being a bag boy seems like a perfect job. My guess is that forty or fifty years of law were enough for your father. My guess is that he doesn't want to spend his time reminiscing and playing checkers with a bunch of "old fogies." Yes, senior activities are great for some people and death to others. Not only should you let him be, you should encourage and support his independence. In another twenty years, he might be ready for the bus trips to the museum.

68.
Single mom working

I'm a twenty-seven-year-old single mom on public assistance. I have two children. One is in school and the other will be going to school next year. According to the law, I have to get a job but this is what I want to do anyway. It will be tough but I should be working and if I have to work I want to be successful even if I have to work in a fast food restaurant. Will the Action Principles help someone like me?

Shaolin Master: This should not be a matter of law. There should be no question that you want to work to make a better life for your children and yourself. Find a job. Do a good job. Find out how to get promoted. Do what you have to do. You will certainly feel better about yourself and your children and friends and family will be proud of you if you are doing your best.

There is dignity in all work. Yes, you can have everything you ever wanted for yourself and your family by working in a fast food restaurant if you follow the Action Principles. Even if you can't start working until next year, you can start reading and studying immediately. This is all about attitude. You can if you think you can. You can with persistence and determination and hard work.

69.
The know-it-all

You seem to have a simple answer for all the questions you're asked. How did you become such a know-it-all?

Shaolin Master: Thank you for calling my answers simple and not simplistic. My secret is to select a question that I can answer. Some of the questions submitted I couldn't answer in a few paragraphs. Many questions I can't answer at all. How can my daughter get into Harvard? How can I raise several million for my great dot COM idea? Why did the drunk driver kill my son?

My goal is not to persuade you to accept my ideas. My goal

is to get you thinking about your own answers. A teacher guides and nudges. You have to do the thinking and studying. When you are thinking and studying to be a better person and to help others, you are a Shaolin Master.

70.
I wish I were a rich man

It seems to me that you put down people with money in favor of cheapskates who want to live a simple life. I don't see anything wrong with earning a healthy salary and having plenty of money to enjoy life. Why are you so against people who want to get rich?

Shaolin Master: Quite to the contrary, the Action Principles encourage you to be successful in all areas of life and this includes making lots of money. Prosperity is one of our "4Ps." And, when you are rolling in the loot, we hope that you will want to make a generous tax-deductible contribution to the American Success Institute.

Being prosperous and living simply is not mutually exclusive. In fact, living simply very often helps lead to the accumulation of wealth. Simply because you're rich doesn't mean that you have to be extravagant and drive a super luxury car, live in a huge mansion and own two hundred pairs of shoes. Simply because you're rich, doesn't preclude you from getting up early to enjoy a sunrise. You still can stop to smell the roses. Your efforts will still be welcomed when you volunteer at a soup kitchen.

By all means, get rich and do good.

71.
Or use your imagination

I live in the inner city and basically have to deal with dirt and grime all day. I haven't got some beautiful tranquil country spot to meditate in. Maybe I could get out to a lake on the weekends but would this be enough time, or how can I be meditating every day?

Shaolin Master: I really don't fully understand your question. Beauty is in the eye of the beholder. Open your eyes and find a daisy; hear a bird sing; see a child's smile. See. Hear. Feel. Taste. Smell. Live. This is meditation. Do you live in a city without parks, churches, colleges and museums? All you need is quiet. Appreciate. This is meditation. Even if you had access to none of these things, you could still imagine. This is meditation.

72.
Born again

My ex-husband was abusive to the kids and me. He left us five years ago and we haven't heard a word from him. Now, he calls and tells me that he's born again and wants to re-establish a relationship, at least, with the kids. The kids want to give their father a chance. What should I do?

Shaolin Master: It sounds like he owes you and your children five years of child support. If he is born again, repayment of his debt and establishment of regular payments should be a good start. In some states, he'd be in jail. If he was a physical abuser, he has a lot of explaining to do. To what does he attribute his problems and how were those problems addressed? What does "born again" mean? Did a minister or counselor help him? Did he have a miraculous vision? Has he been born again for two days or two years?

With those words said, mercy is a powerful human virtue. People can change and turning to religion is often the catalyst. At this point, your primary parental obligation is to the well being of your children and not to him. Go slowly. If he agrees to pay his obligations and if he does sound contrite, a carefully structured reacquaintance alone with you, without the children would be a good first step. Providing his motives and manners are sincere, you can begin to rebuild trust. He may deserve a chance but the ground rules should be well established in advance.

73.
The yin and yang of human nature

My sister goes on dates with one loser after another. She is way too good for these guys. But, when I try to be helpful and talk with her, she gets angry and tells me to mind my own business. Should I just be quiet or is there something that I can do?

Shaolin Master: There is a yin/yang to human nature. It's the teenage mind that wants to rebel and be independent. If you go around bragging to people, "I'm great." They're going to think, "Hey, you're not so great." If you start calling people bums and losers, you put others in a defensive mode to think, "Hey, they aren't so bad." You get the opposite reaction from the one you want.

Try being a reverse psychologist. Find something good in the guy to comment on, his clothes or car or job. You can say, "I see your new boyfriend wears suits. I love men in suits. Don't you?" And your sister may say or at least think, "Sure he wears suits, but I wish he'd get a job to help support his four kids from three previous marriages!" And, if you can find a nice guy and play matchmaker, all she can say is, "No." It's worth a try.

74.
My boss is a bully

I work in a local hardware store and business is bad and getting worse. The big superstores are clobbering us. As sales slip, my boss is getting more and more frustrated and he is more and more often taking it out on his employees, especially me. I don't like it but he's not only the boss, but also the owner. I want to be loyal, but what can I do?

Shaolin Master: Are the superstores hiring? Seriously, you may have to go with the times and seek employment elsewhere. Some local stores have been able to compete successfully against the superstores by finding profitable niche markets and offering better services. If your boss is simply lamenting the "good old days" and cursing his competition, he's got real problems. If he starts to lose good workers with his accusatory behavior, he compounds his problems. You can't change the economy. You can't change your boss. You have no obligation to be loyal to an employer who is not appreciative of your efforts and treats you with disrespect. You can do what's best for you and your family. First, find another job. Second, quit.

75.
Tongue-tied

I work at an upscale restaurant and frequently wait on celebrities. My problem is that whenever I meet someone famous, I get tongue-tied and end up sounding like an idiot. How can I get over this?

Shaolin Master: Winston Churchill would advise you to do what he did which is to picture his audience in their underwear – a great equalizer. Everybody puts his or her pants on one leg at a time. Is the celebrity deserving of your awe or is he or she really awful? Is this person deserving of fame and special treatment? Or, is she just lucky enough to be on television, in the movies or is he lucky enough to be blessed with a 95 mph fastball?

For several years, I worked security at summer concerts and worked for many celebrities. And guess what? Some were down-to-earth, respectful and appreciative and some were spoiled, demanding idiots. Either way, I learned to concentrate on doing my job.

Treat everyone equally. Don't say much. You'll do fine. Remember, they won't know you're an idiot unless you say something inappropriate. Keep the chatter to a minimum. Be a professional and concentrate on your job and provide exemplary service to all your guests.

76.
Another psychology major

I spent four years in college earning a psychology degree and I can't find a job in psychology. Everywhere I apply, it's obvious that they are only hiring people with masters and doctorates. I wish I had known four years ago. I feel like I've wasted those four years. I don't like school enough to go back for two or three more years and just get another degree and probably find myself in the same place. I'm sorry but I just wanted to vent my anger. Can you at least warn others not to major in psychology?

Shaolin Master: Vent your anger at yourself. Go outside and yell, scream and cry and then forgive yourself and get on with your life. It is you as a person that will eventually succeed or fail and not some piece of paper.

Let's help the college students of the world. Let's tell them whether they are majoring in psychology or social work or accounting or political science, to get a job in their chosen fields while they are going to school. Work part-time or summers or get internships or join professional associations or research on the Internet, but find out what being a psychologist or CPA or nurse is all about before you commit four years and a hundred thousands dollars to an education. You must find people already working in your chosen field and talk to them candidly about the plusses and minuses.

Now, what's the job that you would love to have, even if they didn't pay you to do it? Pursue that dream with purpose and passion and you will find prosperity and peace.

77.
Teachers tell me don't teach

I am following your advice and not blindly going down a career path. I wanted to be a teacher, but now I'm not so sure. I spoke with teachers and they all pretty much told me the same thing, "Don't do it." They say that the kids are out of control, that the administration does nothing and the parents blame everyone.

Shaolin Master: I love teaching, and we need good teachers, so I don't want you to give up researching. Unfortunately, some of what you are finding out is true. There are spoiled kids, ineffective administrators and bossy parents. But, there are also plenty of motivated students, motivated principals and motivated moms and dads. Some schools are better than others. Some classes are better than others. If you already have a college degree, try some substitute teaching. If you don't have a degree, try volunteering as a teacher's aide. Again, before you devote your life to a career, try it out. Should you find the schools to be in trouble, perhaps you are being called forward as a leader to start straightening things out. Read your Action Principles and then stand up and tell it like it is.

78.
I'm ugly

My appearance is holding back my career and my social life. I have this feeling that no one wants to be with me. I sometimes feel like I didn't get a very fair deal in life. Are the Action Principles really going to help me?

Shaolin Master: You need a major attitude adjustment. Stop complaining. Walk through a children's ward or the cancer clinic at a hospital and then tell me how important your appearance is. You can buy what you think you need. You can work a little harder and buy yourself designer clothes, cosmetics and even cosmetic surgery.

Beauty is an aura of confidence that shines from the inside. When you feel good about yourself and care about others, people will be drawn to you rather than repelled by you. The Action Principles can do nothing more than to get you to think and you need to start thinking. It is you who will decide if you're the Ugly Duckling or the Beautiful Swan.

79.
I want more forms!

Most brown belts know about eight or nine forms but I know twelve. I know that as a 5th degree black belt, you must know like thirty or forty. I want to learn more but my master says that I have enough forms until I pass my black belt test. This will mean another year of not learning a new form. How am

I supposed to get better? Don't you think this is stupid?

Shaolin Master: Your master teacher realizes correctly that less can be more. Without proper focus, physical technique and correct intent of each move, forms are nothing more than elaborate dance routines. Give me a group of professional dancers and I'll teach them twenty forms in twenty days and to the untrained eye, they will look amazing. You've seen the cardio-kickboxing craze and all the frenzied punches and kicking. Again to the untrained eye, it looks amazing and just like real martial arts. But, there is a lot more to being a skilled warrior than performing a few fancy moves. Your physical skills may be at the brown belt level but your understandings of what it means to be a black belt are immature. Know that if you can perfect one punch and one kick and one blocking system that you will always be able to defeat a dabbler who knows a little about a lot.

80.
Simply no time

My days are very stressful. I have a job and kids and a house. I have a couch potato for a husband. I know that a lot about the Action Principles is simple but I simply haven't got enough time for most of it. What is a harried mother to do?

Shaolin Master: Make sure that you're organized and work from a prioritized to-do list. Assign chores to hubby and the kids. This is a family and you all need to cooperate to get the work done. You probably do get a lot of exercise running around. This may be all you need to stay healthy if you watch your diet. You can mindfully do the dishes and laundry and ironing and cleaning. This can be your meditation and quiet time. You are helping others when you help your kids with their schoolwork. In less than five minutes, you can jot off a note or an email to someone who would love to hear from

you. You can buy flowers for your desk at work and your tables at home. Being a good mother and wife and employee and citizen makes you a follower of the Action Principles and a Shaolin Master. Do your best and there is no more than can be asked.

81.
Haven't spoken in twenty years

Up until about twenty years ago, my brother and I were good friends. Then, he ran off and married the girl that I was going with and we haven't spoken since. Well, last year, he divorced her and I was thinking about calling him. Can I or should I just forget what he did to me?

Shaolin Master: You obviously want to reconnect with him so you have answered your own question and the answer is "Yes." Who betrayed you more, your brother or your girlfriend? At this point, it doesn't matter and talking about it with him won't help either. It is in the past. An easy re-introduction would be to invite him to a family gathering with lots of brothers and sisters and nieces and nephews and where there could be more to talk about than "the topic." I applaud your courage in taking this first step toward reconciliation. Remember the old diplomatic expression, "If you want peace, you have to speak with your enemy."

82.
Capital punishment

I understand that you can feel good about yourself and be politically correct by being against the death penalty. But, how can you say that monsters like Ted Bundy and Timothy McVeigh and John Gacy don't deserve to die for what they did?

Shaolin Master: We must respect life even to the point of letting the monsters that you listed live. We do not do what they did. We do not become what they are.

Many people support the death penalty for the reason that when we say "life without parole" we really don't mean it. We mean, "go to jail and work the system and find a loophole and get out." This saying one thing and meaning another justifiably upsets lots of people. We can and should have life terms that mean first degree murderers leave jail feet first in a pine box and are buried in unmarked graves. For the rest of their natural lives, they can sit in their cells by themselves with a Bible or other appropriate reading and think about their sins and pray to God for forgiveness. Yes, there are crimes that only God can forgive.

83.
Two or three things at once

I attended your seminar "37 Simple Actions" and I was wondering if a person is allowed to combine some of the actions to make sure that you get them all done?

Shaolin Master: You are allowed to do as you please. There is nothing in *The Action Principles* that should be taken as commandments. All the materials are presented as guidelines. For example, "The 37 Simple Actions" are suggestions on how to live the Action Principles and bring more purpose, passion, prosperity and peace into your life. You think about how you can do your best for yourself, your family and your world. Most mornings, I will take a forty-minute walk (1) as I meditate on the day (2). I also carry a small plastic bag with me and I pick up litter along the way (3). Yes, combine at will.

84.
Why not stocks?

I think that the stock market is a good investment but you keep telling people real estate and more real estate. Why not the stock market?

Shaolin Master: Real estate is a great investment and so is the stock market. The key is to save your money, research and take action – invest. Over the last fifty years, the stock market has returned at an annual rate of 12%. At this rate of return, your investments will double every six years. The

Motley Fools and Peter Lynch both offer good practical advice on how to invest safely in the stock market for the long term. The best way to invest in the stock market is to invest based on your personal expertise. Give yourself an edge. If you sell cars, invest in the auto industry. If you are in the insurance business, invest in insurance companies.

85.
With this defining moment

I am setting up a timetable for myself. In two months, I want to stop smoking. In four months, I want to start dieting. In six months, I want to start exercising. Next year, I want to go back to college and finish my degree. In two years, I want to start law school. Does this sound like a good foolproof path to success?

Shaolin Master: Right now, start seeing yourself as the complete person you will soon become. See yourself as that fit non-smoking law student. In this defining moment, become that person. Next, go beyond seeing and start acting, as you will be. See and act your best. Fake it before you make it! This approach may help accelerate your program. This approach may help get you over any rough spots.

Is this a good plan? You know you better than anyone else. Only you can decide to make your plans foolproof. Personally, after half dozen or more tries, I quit smoking at age 40. It was one of the toughest challenges I ever had. Good luck with all your goals.

86.
Pacifism

I don't understand how you can be against capital punishment and still respect all life and not call yourself a pacifist, or are you a pacifist?

Shaolin Master: I am not a pacifist. I believe that there is evil in the world and that unless good people take a stand, evil will triumph. We must remain constantly vigilant and prepared for immediate action. As a soldier, it is kill or be killed to complete the mission. We must support a strong military and take every opportunity we can to thank the veterans who have safeguarded our liberty. We must be sure that our schoolchildren recognize the sacrifices made for freedom.

This is quite different from sparing the lives of captured criminals. We have them. We have stopped the threat. We have won. We can keep them locked up.

87.
Stop the coddling

It seems to me that a lot of the people who ask you questions are whining complainers and that your answers simply coddle them. Why can't you be more honest and direct with them? I think you'd help them a lot more without giving them excuses for their laziness.

Shaolin Master: A Shaolin Master should be a teacher and

72

not a judge. My answers should be simple and direct and action oriented. My answers should be based on the Action Principles. I select questions to answer based on my experience. Many of the questions asked are too narrow and of limited interest to the general readership to be answered on the website.

88.
Environmental fighting

I heard someone say that the only real self-defense was environmental fighting and that this was the style most commonly used by the military. What is it?

Shaolin Master: Bruce Lee was asked his style of karate and he said, "Whatever works." This is environmental fighting, "Whatever works." If you are on a beach, it is using sand and water as weapons. If you are in an office, it is using picking up and throwing a plant or a computer. If you are in a restaurant, it is stabbing someone with a fork. You get the idea. Environmental fighting is using everything in your environment to ensure your victory in the encounter. Are the walls and floors and stairs potential weapons? You bet. Get down. Get dirty. And, please don't forget to bite, gouge, scratch and stomp. Are Special Forces soldiers aware of their environment and alert to all opportunities presented? You bet.

73

89.
Home reinvestment

I took the Master Success Course and I have a real estate question. I live in New York. Can the home reinvestment method work in a big city or does it only work in the suburbs? By the way, I liked the course and learned a lot.

Shaolin Master: I'm glad you enjoyed the course. For the readers who haven't taken the course, here is an overview of the home reinvestment method. You study the market looking for a good deal. You make an offer, buy and occupy the house. You immediately put the house on the market and you live in the house until it sells. You repeat the process. Most home reinvestors look for a return in the 20% -30% range. If, for example, you are buying and selling in the $200,000 range, that's a $40,000 to $60,000 profit which isn't bad for a part-time no hassle real estate investment. A key to this system is to remember that you are looking for a good deal and not your dream house. After a few moves, with a huge downpayment earned, then you can purchase your perfect home or build it. The home reinvestment method should work anywhere. In a big city, you might be buying and selling condos or co-ops rather than single-family houses.

90.
ASI's Action Plans

I see a lot of changes being made to Dojo.com. What kind of plans do you have for the site in the future? I really like the Action Principles and the books, so I'm eager for more. And, I guess you must be busy, so when do you find time to write this column every day?

Shaolin Master: Although we work on the site constantly, changes are usually posted on Monday mornings, EST. I dedicate a few hours every other week to writing columns and will write ten or twelve. However, sometimes a question will come in and I'll get inspired and sit down and write an answer immediately. The questions come from email but also directly from classes I teach and appearances I make.

My goal for Dojo.com is to keep the site fresh and interesting. As broadband expands, you can expect to see more videostreaming. Myself and other masters will be teaching on the site. There will be both free instruction and pay-per-view opportunities. This is probably only two or three years away. We would also like to continue worldwide distribution of the Action Principles and your ideas are certainly welcome. And, as always, we would like to raise as much money as we can for our Central American missions.

91.
Trophies and more trophies

My son who has a blue belt trained very hard for his last karate tournament. He came in fifth in his division and there were only four trophies. He was very disappointed especially since there were 30 competitors in his division, and only eight girls with four trophies in the ten-year-old blue belt girl's divi-

sion. What should I have said to his instructor because this just isn't fair? I feel like asking him for my $20 competition fee back.

Shaolin Master: How about congratulating your son and thanking his instructor for a great tournament performance? Sorry, but you've hit on one of my pet peeves. There are many lessons to learn which far outweigh the value of any trophy. There is the persistence and determination of training. There is the courage to compete. There is the team spirit of competing for your school. There is being proud of having done your best. There is grace under fire. There is good sportsmanship in losing. There is the hope and optimism of learning and coming back to fight again. If your son has learned any of these lessons, you received much more than your twenty dollars worth.

92.
I'm no garbage man

I agree with most of what you have to say in the Action Principles, but walking around picking up trash on the street is where I draw the line. Frankly, I think this is really stupid. I pay taxes to have the streets in my neighborhood clean. I don't see how I better myself by picking up after someone else. I want to respect your judgment, but where did you get this idea?

Shaolin Master: My comment that I pick up litter as I take my morning walk has really gotten to a few people. Unfortunately, even though I live in a nice area, it isn't much of a challenge to fill a small trash bag each morning while I walk. In addition, aside from the litter, bending over a hundred times adds to the exercise benefit of the walk.

This is not about what other people think. This is what I choose to do to make my environment a little bit nicer. I can do this. You do your thing based on your understanding of the Action Principles and I do mine. This is more about my attitude and my perception of myself in relationship to the world, than it is about picking up a few coffee cups and soda cans.

93.
School is stupid

My son is twelve and he is at that age where everything is stupid. I could understand and live with this if it weren't affecting his schoolwork. I'm afraid that he's jeopardizing his future. His grades are slipping and he doesn't seem to care. What can I do?

Shaolin Master: You can ask him how he intends to support himself without a good education. I would drive him through poor neighborhoods. I would point out junky old cars. I would explain to him the pains of low paying jobs. I would make sure that he knew that there would be no fancy vacations, no expensive electronics and few luxuries for his kids. I would tell him to enjoy his life now because it's only downhill from here. This is not being mean. This is reality. This is what life offers to those without initiative. I would engage him in this debate. At the very least, he will be thinking.

Hopefully, he is just going through growing pains and not taking drugs or under the influence of destructive friends. You've got to find out. If this problem persists, he may need professional counseling.

94.
Being the Shaolin Master

I saw your poster, "Be A Shaolin Master." I'm confused. Does this mean that if you do what it says on the poster, you are a Shaolin Master? Is that all you have to do?

Shaolin Master: Live by the seventeen lines of that poster and my answer would be, yes. A master studies, practices, teaches, listens, helps, dares, appreciates, defends and leads. When I experience rude behavior, and I can smile rather than retaliate, I think, "Thank you for giving me the opportunity to be the Shaolin Master." When I am stuck in traffic and I can remain calm, I think, "Thank you for giving me the opportunity to be the Shaolin Master." When I can stop for five minutes and listen to someone with few friends, I think, "Thank you for giving me the opportunity to be the Shaolin Master." You can do the same. You can be a Shaolin Master.

95.
A thief at work

I want to be a good person, but what moral obligation do I have to a private company to tell them that some of their employees are stealing? Frankly, I'm afraid of retaliation and that I'll be the one to lose my job.

Shaolin Master: By virtue of your employment, there is an implied understanding that you will be a loyal employee and act according to the best interests of your company. That's easy to say, but the reality may be a different matter. To your knowledge is the dishonesty limited to a few individuals, an entire department or the whole company? If the whole company is rotten, quit while the getting is good. If it's a department, request a transfer or quit. If it is a few individuals, then consider an anonymous tip to management or security. Is there anyone else at the company in whom you can confide and discuss options? You know the atmosphere at your company. You know if they would welcome a whistle blower or not.

96.
A disabled warrior

I love the military. Sometimes I think that I'm drawn to this career because I'm in a wheelchair and it's never going to happen. OK, I realize that I'll never be accepted, but don't you think that I should be given a chance? After all, there are a lot of jobs that I could do.

Shaolin Master: I strongly agree. If you have the will to serve your country in the armed services, there are many jobs, really most jobs that you are fully capable of doing. Anyone who has seen motivated disabled athletes compete would agree. The British Special Air Service (SAS) that is considered by many to be the finest military unit in the world doesn't turn its back on its disabled. If you are an SAS soldier and disabled on duty, you can stay in the SAS without a leg, arm, eye or two.

Of course, others may not want to call you a soldier, but you can decide to become a warrior. You can earn a black belt. You can teach military science. You can become an advocate for disabled veterans. You can decide to be as tough as any of them and in the process, accomplish a lot.

97.
The Samurai Code

I read this quote in a martial arts book that I don't really understand, it said, "The way of the Samurai is death." What exactly does it mean?

Shaolin Master: The role of the Samurai was to protect and defend his lord even unto death. Accepting death, he would fight fearlessly with no regard for his personal safety. In advanced martial arts training, you would encounter a Japanese phrase "mushin no shin" which means the mind of no mind. In a fight, you have to fight. You can't start thinking about hurting someone else or getting hurt yourself. You can't start thinking about getting sued. You fight. The time to think about the moral and physical ramifications of fighting is before the fight. It is during your training. This is why you learn not to fight because to win you must be prepared to fight all out.

98.
Not a morning person

A lot of the advice you give sounds fine except the getting up positive in the morning. I am a grouch in the morning. Don't talk to me before 9:00 AM. I need a couple of cups of coffee to get going. Is there any problem with my shifting different things like meditation around? I'm really a sweet person at night.

Shaolin Master: Every morning starts a wonderful glorious day that God has given you. If you live your life with purpose and passion, each day will bring you increased prosperity and peace. Take a few deep breaths. Smile. Ask how people are feeling. Play our little game, "Fake it till you make it." Keep

faking it until someone who knows the grumpy you says, "Boy, you seem happy this morning." And you will be happy.

All the rest of the stuff, the exercising and helping others and meditating and looking for beauty in the world can be done at any time of morning, noon or night.

99.
Poor little rich kids

My husband and I are in a financial position that our kids don't have to work. They don't work and I'm starting to get concerned that this may not be a good idea. Should all teens be encouraged to get part-time jobs even if they don't need the money?

Shaolin Master: After college, your kids will get jobs. So, it's not really a question of if they will work but when they will work. The money issues aside, there are many positive lessons to be learned from outside employment. Taking orders. Being punctual. Serving the public. Doing menial tasks. Seeing adult employees interact. Learning different types of jobs. Very simply, independently observing the real world in which they must compete. At the very least, all children should have chores and earn their allowances. At the very least, all children should voluntarily participate in community service activities.

100.
Those cryptic mantras

I'm not a dumb person, but half the time I don't get the mantras. What am I supposed to be learning from them?

Shaolin Master: The idea of the mantra is that they are thought-provoking snippets. They can be aphorisms, sayings, quotations, riddles, tips or tidbits. Some are amusing, some wise and some cryptic. At times, one may make you angry.

Think of them as little poems that float free to the whim of each reader's interpretation. Simply, five readers can have five different opinions. Many teachers, counselors and parents like to use them to stimulate discussion. You write one on the board and then debate the meaning. As you think, you further clarify your personal success philosophy. This is the important point.

The Two Rules of Master Success

1. Improve Yourself. Every day think of small ways to become stronger, more self-disciplined and more self-reliant. Become aware. What are you doing at home, at work or at the gym? What are you doing to train your body and mind? How are your savings and investments doing? What are you doing to make your life more comfortable and peaceful? How are you filling your life with beauty? What are you doing to thank God for all your blessings? Don't let your life pass in a succession of boring days. Small actions done consistently yield tremendous results.

2. Help Others. Listen. Smile. Open doors. Wait your turn. Be patient. Exhibit impeccable manners. Volunteer. Contribute. Be interested and you will be interesting. Be caring and you will have many friends and many customers. You will have a good marriage and good children. You will be respected. You will have found the secret to peace and prosperity.

Shaolin Master's Daily Dozen

1. Read your mission statement.
2. Appear well groomed and organized.
3. Write and prioritize your to-do list.
4. Set aside 20 minutes as quiet time.
5. Exercise for 20-90 minutes.
6. A-B-A-B (Always Bring A Book).
7. Work at work.
8. Be the example.
9. Say a prayer of thanks.
10. Pleasantly surprise someone.
11. Find a small way to spoil yourself.
12. Maintain awareness.

Shaolin Master's Business Rules

Success in business isn't necessarily complicated. Whether you work for yourself or others, through diligent application of the following simple rules, you are putting yourself on the fast track to prosperity.

1. Offer a quality product or service that the market demands at a fair price.

2. Appreciate your customers. Say thank-you, follow-up and ask for more business and referrals.

3. Copy success. Find the industry leaders who are already doing what you want to do and do what they are doing. In most situations when you are establishing your business, it makes more sense to be imitative rather than innovative.

Write Your Action Principle

"These Action Principles belong to everyone. We need your experience, knowledge and insights to make the Action Principles truly representative of those universal values and codes of conduct to which we should all endeavor to promote through our example."
- Bill FitzPatrick

Try your hand at writing an Action Principle and share your positive thoughts, insights, knowledge, experience and special talents with your fellow Action Principles Champions and the world. Instructions for writing and posting your Action Principle are on Dojo.com.

Translators Needed

We need translators willing to volunteer their skills to bring the Action Principles to the world as a free ebook. Upon completion, you will receive acknowledgement on the site, signed copies of all our books and a small honorarium. And, of course, you'll have the satisfaction of helping us to help others. Further information provided on Dojo.com. And, thank you!

Be a Shaolin Master

Study – Practice – Teach

Work Free of Praise or Criticism

Stand Confidently

Appreciate All Life

Seek Simple Solutions

Listen to Learn

Test Strictly

Match Words with Actions

Strive for Excellence

Assume the Lead

Dare To Risk

Defend the Defenseless

Proceed Patiently

Organize Methodically

Find Beauty Everywhere

React Calmly

Live Simply in the Now

Commit to *The Action Principles*

Smile Contentedly

Dojo.com

If you're a martial artist, you'll love this site.

If you stand on principles, you'll love this site.

If you're a peace advocate, you'll love this site.

If you're self-reliant, you'll love this site.

If you want to retire early, you'll love this site.

If you like free stuff, you'll love this site.

Really, if you like this book, you'll love this site!

◆ Books ◆ Videos ◆ Posters ◆ Classes ◆ Music
◆ Columns ◆ Speeches ◆ Seminars ◆ Merchandise
◆ And, lots, lots more.

Accept this Action Challenge

Single copy (signed)	$6
10 copies	$35
100 copies	$250
1,000 copies	$2,000
10,000 copies	$15,000

Join us in promoting the spirit of *The Action Principles*™. Begin by giving copies of this book to: family members, friends, clients, customers and co-workers. If you can, please consider doing more. Make a positive contribution in your community by distributing multiple copies of this book to: schoolteachers, counselors, police officers, social workers, clergy members and others who are in a position to share *The Action Principles*™ with those most in need.

Corporate Sponsorship

Inspire your employees, your customers, your community.

We will work with you to custom print copies of *The Action Principles*™. Your CEO can write an introduction to the book and your corporate message can be displayed on the back cover. You can handle distribution through your outlets or we will assist in arranging distribution to suit your marketing objectives.

Memorial Editions

Do you have a loved one who lived a life exemplified by the Action Principles? We will custom print copies of the Action Principles dedicated to the memory of your loved one. At your option, we will ship the books to you or donate and distribute them on your behalf.

Note: Customization is available for printings of 10,000 copies or more.

To order online: Dojo.com.

To order by telephone: 1-800-585-1300

By mail: ASI, 5 North Main Street, Natick, MA 01760

International: E-mail us regarding postage,
info@dojo.com

Please Join Us In Our Work

The American Success Institute (ASI) is a 501(c)3 non-profit educational and philanthropic organization founded in 1993 by Bill FitzPatrick. The mission of ASI is to promote principle based personal development. Each year, ASI donates tens of thousands of motivational books to schools, correctional facilities and social agencies. We also support missionary activities in Central America.

We need and appreciate individual donations in any amount. With a credit card, please call 1-800-585-1300 or make a donation to ASI on-line at Dojo.com. Checks can be mailed to ASI at 5 North Main Street, Natick MA 01760. Donations are tax deductible. Please verify your particular tax situation with your accountant. If your company is involved in charitable giving or matching donations, please ask them to consider our organization.

Thank you in advance for your help and generosity.

Speeches, Seminars, Clinics, Classes, Appearances

Bring the wit and wisdom of
Bill FitzPatrick to your next event!

This is easy. If you like *The Action
Principles™*, you will like Bill's presentation. If you like the *Master's
Meditation Mantras*, the Ask a Master
columns, the books, the videos and
the Dojo.com website, you will like
Bill's presentation. Bill has been a
teacher for over thirty years and has
given hundreds of speeches. Your audience will have a
great time. They will leave the event smiling, motivated and
thanking you. GUARANTEED.

Topics: For a list of suggested topics, go to Dojo.com.

Contact: We are very happy to work closely with you to
make your event a success. Call Jessica Plachy for more
information, a demo tape and available dates. Call at
800-585-1300 or email her at jesse@dojo.com.

The Action Principles

1 copy.............$6
10 copies $35

Sports Legends On Success

.......................$6

100 Action Principles of the Shaolin

The first edition - signed copy....$6

Tenga Una Actitud Positiva

.......................$6

Master Success

.......................$19.95

100 Action Principles of the Shaolin

Illustrated edition - $12.95

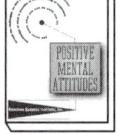

Positive Mental Attitudes

.......................$6

Ask a Master

Volume 1 ....$6
Volume 2 ....$6

African-Americans On Success

.......................$6

Master's Meditation Mantras

Volume 1 ....$6
Volume 2 ....$6

Action Principles Posters

Single poster $6
Ten assorted (may contain duplicates) $10

CDs

Shaolin Master Music One...............$20

Shaolin Master Music Two...............$20

To order online: Dojo.com
To order by telephone: 1-800-585-1300
To order by mail: ASI, 5 North Main Street, Natick, MA 01760
International: Please order books through Amazon.com.

About Bill FitzPatrick

Bill FitzPatrick is a teacher. He enjoys a reputation as a popular martial arts master, small business expert and popular motivational speaker. Bill is an Eagle Scout and served for six years as Infantry Sergeant in the Army Reserve. He earned a Master's Degree in Education from Boston College. He is a 5th degree black belt in Shaolin Kempo karate and has taught self-defense classes for over twenty years. For fifteen years, Bill ran a high school program for court offenders in Cambridge, Massachusetts. He has written extensively on real estate investing, small business, personal performance and martial arts topics. Bill is the Founder and Executive Director of the nonprofit American Success Institute (ASI). His speaking engagements and charitable work on behalf of ASI have taken him throughout North and Central America, Europe, Asia and North Africa. He is the author of ten books including *The Action Principles™* and *Master Success*. Bill lives with his wife Karen in a Boston suburb. Bill and Karen are the proud uncle and aunt to many wonderful nieces and nephews.